The Magda Poem Cycle

POEMS FROM THE SOUL FOR THE SOUL

Dawn Richerson

Poetry Books from the Soul for the Soul

© 2024 Dawn Richerson

THE MAGDA POEM CYCLE

Poetry Books from the Soul for the Soul

ISBN #978-1-942969-78-5 softcover
ISBN #978-1-942969-79-2 e-book

The poems in this collection were written between 1997 and 2024. These poems are a part of the "Magda Cycle" of poems connected to long-remembered soul memories. Some appear in *Testament: 12 Books of Love and a Single Story [A Half-Life in Poems]* which include collected poems by the author.

All rights reserved. No part of this publication may be reproduced, distributed or transmitted in any form or by any means, including photocopying, recording, or other electronic or mechanical methods, without the prior written permission of the publisher, except in the case of brief quotations in reviews and certain other noncommercial uses permitted by copyright law. For permission requests, contact the author through the website below.

AUTHOR WEBSITE
https://DawnRicherson.com

Contents

Introduction

Piece by Peace
More Than Pieces 4
I Should Have Liked to Have Been Invited 6
Present to Promise 8
A Dream, Alive 10
Dream of the Dolphin Days 13
To Ride on the Wave of the Wind 14
I Have Become the Flame 16

The Jesus Story
33 Lines: This Sacred Chalice That We Share 18
It Is a Miracle We Live 20
Shaken Loose 22
The Way You Must Imagine: First Recollection 24
In the Fullness of the Light 25
The Way You Washed Your Hands 26

Conversations with Paul
Notes on Tribulation 30
The World That Was Built 32
Eternal Tribute and What Remains 36
The Distance 38
Conversion 42
Follow the River's Flow 45
What Still There Is to Gain 47
Witness 49
Some Home for Freedom 51
Context 54
In Egypt or in Greece 56
Your Shame Is Not My Shame 58
Good Grief 60

Evidences 62
She Who Loves and Watches Over Me 65
Back to Italy 66
Desert Moon 68
The Wreckage Lies Behind 69
Where We Meet Again 70
If I Have to Move Mountains 72
Shall I Go to India 73
I Will Shoot No Arrows 75
Stacks of Books 76
There Is More 78
After the Storm 81
News of Your Release 86
All Ships Have Sailed 89
In the Shadow of My Mountains 92
All That Shall Not Be Taken 95
One Last Ship 98
These Three Remain 101
Laid Bare..103
On the Way 104
All the Things I Know Nothing Of...........................107
Michael, Mary, and Me 110

The Coming Age Now Here

A Tick Tock Truth 114
Shot in the Heart, He Returns the Arrow of Love 116
Walls Come Tumbling Down: After Revolution 117
What Must Be Faced..118

Introduction
The Magda Poem Cycle
Eternal Seasons

The Magda Poem Cycle

This series of poems is partial both in terms of what is shared publicly and also in terms of my own partiality as the poet toward portions of the Magda story that has so long been alive in me. With that acknowledged, I want to share my soul intent as the poet and author these words. The intent is twofold.

First, as it relates to my soul's own unique journey through this life, I must express these things. To not release this flow would be to damn myself to eternal suffering. And, in spite of having chosen it so many times in my life, I do not believe in suffering. I believe in the eternal season of love and life lifted, and humanity with it, into the Realm of Radiance.

Second, and far more in service to the whole, is the intent to set all things free for, in the word of Paul who knew so much of the nature of true freedom, it is for freedom we have been set free. You can read Paul's discourse on freedom in Galatians 5:1 in the Bible. As for my own experience here in this life it is that I choose to fly free and to only fly for freedom. In other words, the path of freedom is the compass I use to navigate the seasons of this life.

But there is more. I carry in my heart the love she who lives there had for all hearts and the many rivers that flow through those hearts. That love I cannot leave unexpressed. Though my own conviction is that there are many here who remember her and carry threads of her timeless tapestry of truth, this does not mean that I can forfeit the strand of her story I know so well, no matter how heretical. I come by this naturally. She always laughs with me, for it seems so did she.

So it is for my own freedom and for the freedom of humanity, which is both a freedom from and a freedom for, that I write. These are poems from the soul for the soul. They are for all time and all whose hearts are freed in timed. With so much love, Dawn

Piece by Peace
The Magda Poem Cycle
Winter and a Frozen Season

More Than Pieces

Here is her hand.
There is her foot.

Here you can stare at her skull
encased in thick glass—

behind bars
as the church likes to keep her,

Though now with purported admiration
and some measure of veneration.

But what you have missed
in the pomp and circumstance

is that she is forever faithful, free
from being tied to your circuitry.

She is alive and I love her.
I am alive and she loves me.

So mix her up and make of her
what you will. Seek your definition.

But know her joy in seeing all things risen
will not be contained, cajoled, controlled.
Feast if you will. Seek her prayers should you choose.
Know more than pieces of she you seek to break or use.

There is no denial of a testimony that rings,
true as the bells of a holy matrimony:

"I have seen the Lord!"
Word and flesh birth worlds.
Two who belong to each other,
for eternity, to this revelation of a mystery.

I Should Have Liked to Have Been Invited

I should have liked to have been
invited to my own party,
to have walked among you, my friends.
I invite you now to celebrate in my stead.

I should have liked to have been showered
with a thousand kisses,
but I only dreamed of your lips. Kiss now
those golden shores to which you make your way.

I should have liked to have been bestowed
with baskets of roses.
Still, the skies parted in my dream:
the world was born, everything coming up roses.

I should have liked to have received some
thank you for being here,
nod of acknowledgement for love's
labor. I welcome you with joy. It matters not.

I should have liked for the message
to have been received in time—
for it to have been my time, our
time just one time. For all time, I will share my love.

The Magda Poem Cycle

I should have liked to have given more
and received more in kind.
I open my heart to receive
now this gift, divided, multiplied, blessed, broken.

Present to Promise

Never mind long stretch of empty,
agony of uncertainty,
all who've gone too soon from her life,
floods of ever grey day.

Opportunity has arrived
right on time. This bird is ready
to fly out of a gilded cage
through the westward-facing

Wonder window to her new world
that has waited through many years
to receive her heart's buoyant song
and come back to life. Now!

Now knows the future is right here,
emerging from a clear blue sky
like lightning splitting a darkness
that has lingered too long—

Like shooting arrows, golden rays
of morning pierce her soul
to reveal a valley of peace,
a tenderness in time

And a time out of time. Now, when
there are beginnings at the end

of a winding gravel road, hope
rises like a lost song.

Present to promise, she stands strong
in circle of recreation,
to which we are born and belong,
dances free with the wind.

A Dream, Alive

Alive, I am swept up
in the dream of a world
where candlelight gives ambience
to receive long-lost dreams ready now
to fly fast to me, where fireflies keep alive
in me a magic jar full of the dreams
that never die.

I know this heartfelt invitation.

She calls me to the morning, into
the lightness of a feather dream
where I gaze into the kaleidoscope
that changes colors, settling
softly into stillness, where

Through a stained-glass blessing
I become the morning rose,
open to sun and find I am
yet alive, born in the seed
of a dandelion dream.

In this world, the wind blows
and all life swirls, slowly at first,
like bubbles breathed with blessing
into a summer's day and then
the pace quickening, wind

wrapped around me with a force
of grace that touches me within and
rustles ten thousand rainbow leaves
that scatter like stars.

A trinity of truth, the turbine turns
on the mountain top and I drift away,
a feather in the sky, forgotten question
blowing in the wind. I move into
the current and the current
moves through me, breathing life into all
the dying things, awakening in me

what has slept through long winter,
summer breeze of yesteryear.

In this world sounds morph and magnify
then fade to muffled meaning
that slips away—but that's OK,
for there is no longer need
for interpretation, only moving
to the music of a higher love,
things above settling.

Softly in this world below
people come and people go, move
like magic rainbows sliding into
fields of gold on an autumn day
that feels like spring, season
of beginning.

In this world wishes don't have to
come true because they have
always been alive in me
and everyone can see
the way they multiply

on a blustery beautiful day
that never ends

because the wind
ever begins again.

In this world color changes rapidly
with the wishes of the moment—

a poem, a prayer, a promise,
like a whispered breath

of being here where
I am

a dream, alive...
a dream alive…
a dream alive…

Dream of the Dolphin Days

Long the luxurious line of time
and I a dancer of delight sailing on,
ever in process

as the transportation,
certain transformation,
sure transubstantiation,

heart broken, soul open,
a life poured out
for all to see—

ever upside down, then turned
the right way round; these true thoughts
bubbling up, surf side signposts,
real and remnant reminders

that life has been the boat
and I afloat
thanks to you three—

the one who walks ahead,
the one who walks behind,
the one who walks beside,

trinity rising
from the open sea, ever within the heart
of our tumultuous journey home.

To Ride on the Wave of the Wind

It is now as it was then, was then
as it is now. Though I feel small, unworthy,
weary from my journey through time
and this strange solace, this life of mine,
Still there is but one thing true, tried
through and through. It is not a mighty strength,
for though hers has held me and kept me and,
while I may at times carry her sword of truth,

Planted in my heart, its comfort slipped from me
long ago. Or perhaps I fell beneath its weight.
Maybe it is the lack of strength, after all,
that led me to trust this one thing even more.
Not strength, but surrender—a willingness,
some might say a fool's errand, to climb and climb,
to come right to the edge of all I know and,
having made the journey to some pinnacle,

To dive! To leap into the arms of life
and trust I will be carried on the winds
to where I am meant to be. And then, again,
to rise when I feel a battered ram or made to be

A battering ram, wrongly used, misperceived,
twisted out of shape beyond all recognition.
To know myself as something other than
this ugliness cast upon me. I rise, I rise

And learn to ride on the wave of the wind
and dare to dance with it until I believe I too have
wings to fly. And if I fall, then learn to swim, buoyed by
the oceans deep. And then to find dry land.

I suppose this could be seen as lunacy, but it is
the only thing that keeps me sane. I am alive
in a full moon dream from which I would wake you
to see the truth of love you have never seen in me.

I Have Become the Flame

I have walked through the threefold fire
and I have become the flame.

Wonder, Mystery and Beauty—
these three have been my true friends.

When all others pointed fingers
or have fallen, fallen away,

sun, moon and stars have stood with me
in last remains of this day.

So closes the curtain tonight,
so falls sudden sword of light.

All-consuming creative pow'r
rises in this final hour,

and still I stand alone in love.
just another burning tower.

The Jesus Story
The Magda Poem Cycle
Spring and Innocence

33 Lines: This Sacred Chalice That We Share

So maybe—after so many passages
through the stone archways of time
and up one grassy slope or another—
maybe, even still, it is true
that there will be love
because Love
is all there is.
And more:

Somewhere, perhaps—
in fields of lavender or a forest
of barren trees bursting full with light—
will come a moment of radiance, transcendent
and the stunning realization that, maybe,
even as I searched everywhere, passing
through a thousand doors in time,
turning the world upside down,
turning myself inside out,
giving my whole heart
to follow, follow you,
you were with me
all the while and I
now, here,
with you.

So maybe—standing still in the clearing
in the breath between what's next
and the miracle heartbeat of this now—
maybe, even still, it is true
that I am held in love
because Love
is who I am.
And more:

It Is a Miracle We Live

It was a miracle we lived—
What we felt a desert barren
where all was lost to time
became wellspring of promise, pure
waters of life flowing freely
into humanity.

From far distance, we bear witness
to bountiful harvest of fruit
from humble olive tree,
our hearts laid bare by age of peace,
long-awaited sign of our spring
and the white dove's return.

We step forth into a new world,
born because we are and have been
laid out, pressed, perfected,
wholly formed, transformed completely
into blessed love we once knew.
I was blind and now see:

when you turned water into wine,
it was a sign of things to come,
of who we were to be;
yet, we could scarce have held it then—
a truth so vast and beautiful,
required expansion.

"New wineskins," you said. We knew not
you spoke of our own expansion,
blessed capacity
to become vessels filled with love,
multiplied in remembrance,
wed now to present joy.

It is a miracle we live.

Shaken Loose

Something happens to us when truth is unveiled
and everything turns on its head.
The lamb becomes lion; the lion, a lamb,
and we are shaken loose, released
to take up the sword and do harm or to run,
to swear that we never knew you
or to be caught up in seeming injustice,
swept away in the sands of time.

It is unsettling when day breaks and the dark
drama drags on and we buckle
beneath this world's crushing weight. The veil is torn,
within as without, and we see
that while we have always believed in your dream,
now we are invited to live—
to be the whole of who we are, unhindered,
and step full into our story.

In centuries that followed after the end
and strange new beginning again,
we stumbled, tripped up by the upside-down,
inside-out Way of Love. Shaken
by a freedom so vast, we shackled ourselves
to one fragment of truth or
the other and, not meaning to, diminished
the freedom for which we have been

set free. We are remembering, coming back,
waking up in this Great Return
and turning again to the truth that something
happens to us and we are changed,
brought back to life. We stand at the entrance to
an empty tomb, not belonging
to it, waking to the realization
that, alive, we are free to love—

Loosed from all the ties that bind, we are woven
into expanding tapestry
that welcomes all the colors of who we are
or have ever been. Shaken loose,
All else falls away.

The Way You Must Imagine: First Recollection

The Way—"You must imagine!"
you would say, "It always opens up."

I come across the stone tablet in the tangled woods.
Here, there is no writing on the wall, save
the mark of time and our story rising up.
I follow and imagine, imagine, imagine
you will meet me here.

First I see you, laughing at all these wonders,
so many signs along my way. I remember
the way the light flickers in your eyes,
golden brown and speckled with the remnant,
verdant forest filled with fractals of eternity.

Next, flashes fast the tomb and stone, you,
simple gardener in disguise, and I beside
and all that flashed before my eyes
that morning we met again, everything
changed, between us, for all life.

I think of the way you still imagine me,
standing here, strong and silent, musing
at this signpost that reminds me
of a thousand missing stories,
our life's sacred mystery.

In the Fullness of the Light

How radiant shines
that light whose streams burst
the dam of despair and flood
the familiar room full with

  love's rising hope.

See how it gathers –
flowing in from roads
long since traveled, pushing through
the pinhole crack of soul

  where all the faith

That's left is enough,
inexplicably,
to fill the basket of days
and light twelve candles

  for those yet on their way.

The Way You Washed Your Hands

You were always washing your hands.
Cleanliness next to godliness, I suppose.
You told me once you liked things clean,
no matter the heart of a thing.

Fairness, they said, was your virtue.
A man of honor, reason, and good measure,
you wanted peace and the rule of law;
that much we felt and saw.

I saw the light pass through your eyes
and the cloak of sadness that chased it down.
I saw you shudder, then turn and leave the scene
when others forced a thorny crown.

It would all go as you said it should go.
Of that there was never any question.
Later you would recite by rote all the reasons why
and say you had no part in how it went down.

You had not torn his clothes.
You had not thrust the spear.
You made the difficult choice, for the best.
You had no part in all the rest.

There was much on your plate
and you would say after, "It was simply too late."
And so, all entanglements aside,
you simply let the people decide.

In your heart I saw and felt
who you knew yourself to be, but it was only
ever the way you washed your hands
that has lived for lifetimes inside of me.

Conversations with Paul
The Magda Poem Cycle
Summer and the Burning Sun

Notes on Tribulation

True tribulation and meaning muddled…
these are days that trouble me. It is the cause
and not effect that invites our focus now.

The reversal of current flows faster
by the day as all those who burn
for all they thought that was
and evermore should be
turn so willingly
to trade sovereignty

for a booster shot of confidence,
blind it seems to the coming chasm
created by a problem-solution continuum
that seems so plausible, believable, but turns
pure Love into false battlefield and
desecrates this sacred heart—

our home, given by grace
but seized fast by those
who would so easily
dictate our comings
and goings and
fix us in place.

This is the beginning of sorrows
he spoke about, the waxing cold.

I remember when you made your argument
persuasive as always before the council.
I remember James. I remember how
I grieved a thousand deaths before
your death and then the temple
was destroyed. I remember how

such silence fell upon us, how some
among us saw too late their fate
at having made a fool's bargain
in the basement where a Church was born
where money changed hands, quickly,
so like his kiss, a betrayal by cover of night.

History repeats itself.
This world fades for me.

Thy Kingdom come.
Thy will be done.

The World That Was Built

In that higher aspect
from which you lived
for such a sliver of time
and to which I clung, dangling
from the waning light of hope
that in the fullness of time
you would yet remember,
there was the glimpse of golden.

There was everything
one could ever dream—
a world, pristine; love,
magnified; all things
coming back to life.

But even he, alive in you,
chose to await your choice
rather than to choose
for you. How he held
your heart! How I too
loved you.

All that was possible then,
as now... how the world shook
with recognition of its purity!
I wonder sometimes if it is
not completely lost to you,
having sealed yourself

inside a tomb, which is nothing
that he or I or any aligned with life
would ever want for anything
or anyone. But ten thousand echoes
of my pleas for intervention
and a second resurrection
were left unanswered
and your ringing ears
seemed not to hear what
your heart knew but which
you buried all the more.

You chose, a million times over,
then and now, there and here,
construction, the meaning
of which is to heap up, to devise,
to form in the mind some
better world you would offer
and for eons have worked
to polish and present as truth:
rigid religiosity and spinning systems
devoid of the true life you cast down—
twelve stars from the crown scattered,
like stars that fell from the sky—
and you no longer desiring to belong
to the love you are.

Love has not languished.
It has lived upon the land,
rising up like smoke signals,

clear messages left for you
and all who followed,
immaculate meaning you have,
it seems, chosen again
to disregard.

Does this false, constructed world
now finally hold full sway, in the way
that you can no more reach the love
alive in you, far beyond the construct
of egoic rage born long ago, far away,
and also close to here and now
of the seed of rancid fear planted
to control what would grow
in a field of plenty?

In the prism of the last tear
there was the world I held
for the millennia, choosing
then as now to remain
with all that is true nature
and not a manufacture.
And so the realm
of radiance
begins.

There is a rising:
four words that were the last
I ever spoke to you in that time
you so easily left behind
and all the things you killed
to construct the world as you
would have it. Now, again,
I live them, walking with faith
in the way he taught us
to receive.

And dare to dream
that I might still believe.

Eternal Tribute and What Remains

She laid the flowers on his grave today
before the thundering rains arrived to match her cries
ringing through the valley and a deluge of grief
washed all that came before away.

Yesterday, the day she buried him, something died
in her forever; yet, wherever life will lead her as it
surely will—and just as surely as she will follow still,
he is raised to life and runs free in her heart.
Her heart will yet survive where her ravaged
mind and savaged body may not. As does his,
which lives and beats and makes its home here:

> *This is the Love that remains*
>
> and will not be buried but is set free:
> butterfly being.

The day she was worried sick she could not
have imagined cruel twist of fate and metal, a devil's
snare or bargain, attempt to bribe or bait most beautiful
of souls—death unleashed like venom, spewed forth

like taste of the vomit in her mouth moments after
her body's rejection of rancid falsehood, at what
her eyes and his were forced to see, at what
we had all been forced to swallow, a myriad

of mirrored moments mashed up. Her sickness at the death
of innocents slaughtered or seized—all who like him fell silent
in a swoop. She howled for hours when he could not.

Hear her now:

> *This is the Life that rises*
>
> and does not sleep, a dream that never dies,
> soothes her, stills her cries.

Thin threads, she thought, were all she had left,
having been again lowered into hell and her hold
on hope, already frayed, though fervently through
six days and nights she prayed, pouring out petition

And blessing, calling on legions of angels, a light brigade
to cradle him, bring him home to her. The way the last
golden glow glimmered on the clouds that sunset
he was missing before she found him mangled, the way
the light traced the line of the tree where they had sat,
dressed in life's finest hues just days before…
he spoke to her then, saying:

> *This is the Light that shines*
>
> a rainbow through woven web of wonder,
> hollowed, hallowed now.

The Distance

With all due honor for the truth of who you are
and all the ways our storied hearts are woven as one,
I will suffer no more of your falsity. Nor will I continue
to intervene on your behalf with a higher authority
when you chirp on about integrity even as you
go on and on running in circles seeking to convince
yourself you were right or you did not know
or you could not see or you are not free
or this just can't be. Enough of such
disreputable dishonor in the name
of diligence.

Funny, not funny, how I who only had love
was the target of such vile and vitriol and all
the silencing while you bustle about or twist and shout
to all the oohs and aahs. They join your game
and ooze their shame and project it all
on me. You may be shipwrecked but
what do they care, for somewhere—*"Look!*
She's over there!! Speaking up when she should be silent."—
they say there is the one who could kill our story
with her penchant for the truth. Truth be told,
I never did then or now. I followed the river's flow.
Many rivers flow, even here when I know the cost
and nearly lost my life and lost so many things.

But from a distance rings in my ear
shallow, empty praise paired with his name,
he who walks with me and talks with me.

The Magda Poem Cycle

It strikes me in the heart this time and not
my head. Here I am far from dead.

If you should speak another word
about me as if I were an object or a thing
or enter into another deliberation
steering said concerned conversation
in any manner that you choose,
whomever's family you may dare
to engage, whatever so-called community
which long ago excluded me you gather,
they still so adored with all the reasons why
I am to be ignored—if, then from this day forth,
the reversal of fortune in truth
shall commence.

Do mark the date this February
on the 5th for it has significance.
Do you not know? Have you not heard?
Listen, listen to the little bird, for the one
who tells me everything shall now fly to you
as the hawk shall sound his cry and descend
one way or the other.

Their two-sentence letter made them feel better
and was delivered with a stamp, unlike the first
stuffed into the box by deacon deliverer
scurrying straight from the gates of hell,
a toll of the bell 23 years ago.
Where did the time go?

The Magda Poem Cycle

Two years now since the line of demarcation
and decision returned and my heart decimated
placed back in my hands. Life has its demands;
still I would bear all things, believe all things, hope
all things, endure all things. I am granted this: a wish,
and I have made mine. It is that neither you
nor any soul who tears at the whole shall be
permitted to speak that name of One who
touched my eyes so I could see and go forth into all
to remember again who I am, the One who lived
in you as life itself, somewhere still does.

In case you have not noticed, all
premeditated harm has been returned
unopened but with the bill for damage done
plus interest due from all who hide in deciding
from a distance the direction one should take.

Shake, shake, shake. All shall be shaken
and seen for what it is. Whether they share
my blood or wish to see it spill, whether
in their shame-soaked stupor they fling fire,
spurred on by devils flying in the sanctuary
or sit like ducks, twelve men lined up, dumbstruck
by your powers of persuasion in a room where
you sit satisfied and speak with silver tongue
as if I were no one and not even there.

No weapon forged against me will prevail,
but only time will tell true colors and false flags
and all the pomp and circumstance around

the pied piper's hollow tune and all those
who followed suit. The emperor indeed
has no clothes and I suppose, if this is the way
you want the story to go, then this is how it will go.

As for me, your letter is written on my heart
and nothing will part me from it or erase it
from the record, whatever you may do and
wherever it is done, from three feet behind
or from a distance—this gap, this gulf created
by the chasm and vacuous void in which
you place yourself again and again.

The old world passes now.
A new life begins.

Conversion

But the Lord said to Ananias, "Go! This man is my chosen instrument to proclaim my name to the Gentiles and their kings and to the people of Israel. I will show him how much he must suffer for my name."
Acts 9:15-16

When one undergoes a change
from one form to another, whether struck
at once by blinding light and just as quickly
the sudden dark or having been immersed
in the liquid light of a love made manifest
for eons, they may only then come to realize
the solution everywhere all at once
after so long a dissolution...

This conversion is a shaking loose
of all that had seemed so right and true.
Lesser versions, per your former self's belief,
are seen in the light of day as a horror.
You grieve all the diversions and dichotomies,
divisions of your soul and see it clearly now,
how the inversion seemed mere oversight,
the transposition of two tiny letters in a word.

What once appeared to be subversion—
a thing to be stopped at all costs, cut off
at the head, called out and dressed up,
whether with some scarlet letter or a gold star,
marked as an infidel or made into an object lesson

in some grown-up show and tell while playing
self-appointed defender, clansman of the clean-up crew;
these same people, places, things, are now seen
in a different light and having undergone
some strange reversion.

They become stark reminder of the necessary
reliance on a work of grace and that grace,
at times, a terror that if not tended to becomes a thorn,
that if not acknowledged and honored lodges
deep in the soul and then makes a gash
through which we fall in time—
the dream, yours and mine, lost
at so great a cost to so many.

So despite the moment of conversion
there is no sweet surprise, some moment of salvation
at which one world is switched for another.
There is no escaping who and what we were;
besides, all of us have one thorn or another.
And yet, for the one who dares the journey on,
leading with the heart's conviction, resting in
the grace of a terrible reckoning without seeking

to control—for this one there is so great a gift
of transformation that the world might shift upon its axis
and still the Love can no more be taken from you
than the truth of what remains can be shaken in me.
This, then, is the Law: mystery, work of grace that is
a mercy, an all-consuming fire that sets all things

spinning and finds in bittersweet endings
fought against so long a new beginning
this world has yet to see and, too,
the reclamation of a dream:

a white rose that blooms
and rises from the grave.

Follow the River's Flow

This morning the heavens opened
to grant me this reprieve,
to pour out light upon the land,
to give you second sight,

to reveal sycophants and serpents
all around, to heal your heavy heart
with sacred sound, to send eternal echoes
so that you may see and know

falsity of "friends," their treachery in full.
From the left and from the right
swinging scythes shall separate
the wheat from chaff, pompous people

dressed up as something they are not.
Pay attention to the slip of tongue
and the Evil One slithering there,
whispering words of supposed care.

You, too, who read this now beware
for there is no escape. Shed now your cape.
Return to grace in which we together are held,
before having forfeited your soul you too are felled.

Portent of this peril and potent prophecy
came swift this morning with sun's ascent.
Call it distant possibility if you will but, still,
feel the sincerity with which I offer it up

and fill your cup with love and honesty.
See the desolation you have created,
true teachers you have berated. Then go.
Leave this land. Do not look back.

Follow the river's flow.
You will find me there
and I will be happy
to welcome you.

What Still There Is to Gain

When you were a child
you talked like a child,
you thought like a child,
you reasoned like a child.

And then you became a man
and in time came face to face with
the man in the mirror, reflected too
by my cloud-like appearance.

Three things remain.
We shall see face to face
in the moment they return,
gushing forth from within

like the river running wild
where you laughed as a child
and I first saw you, seeing I
had jumped too late. Later,

I would watch you walking through the gate
without me, listening to my favorite song,
thinking it all wrong and dooming myself
to the dungeon life. But I never forgot

the better part—first when you put me
in my place calling me the clanging cymbal;
but you also judged me wrong, for I had
a greater love than you dared imagine.

Love delights not in evil. It rejoices
with the truth. It perseveres.
Love keeps no record
of wrong and in its pure light

all partiality fades. What comes clear
is what we knew as little children
when the spark was a flame that
could be called by no other name

than Love. To this we may return.
And this time no man nor beast nor
man-made emperor nor charlatan
shall dare to take it from us.

Now, as then, love never fails
and there is everything to gain.
The door is open as before and
He calls to us to come as little children.

Witness

You, who will live forever,
and not only in my heart, who
will no doubt keep the faith
and fight the good fight,

hear me and know:
whatever loss I may have had
I will count it gain, knowing
I will see you once again
in the great beyond.

I am the rose fading faster
than I had first imagined.
Perhaps by some miracle
all will be laid to rest within me

and love raised up to lift me.
For that joy set before us,
so much was endured
and set aside.
Of this I am certain:

you will add concluding exhortations
and I will not mind it, for they will be
fine words and you are deserving
of that word, last or first, first or last.

What did it really matter?
Forgetting what is behind...
in this much we are in agreement.
Yet, I cannot press on.

I do not know that I can carry on
even through unto that day I love.
I shall be with them—great cloud
of friends and witnesses.

In the wind and in the rain
I will meet you on the way.

The Magda Poem Cycle

Some Home for Freedom

Waiting on the God of my salvation,
I wonder, do you consider still
these present troubles nothing
in light of what will be?

I held long to your promise.
How many eons? And was it
not you who spoke it too
before the age you wrote it?

Babel and the noise of confusion
that followed would hold me captive,
even standing strong, one of two
as two together with the holy One.

Yet this one thing I was granted:
to know within my heart that I am free,
to know it so completely that even in
this endless captivity, I am not bound

to any singular pursuit or defined
by the boundaries men have made.
Though I appear a prisoner, forlorn,
my life whittled down to nothing,

still I walk by faith through a desert dream
seeing rivers multiply, seeking only

to let this Love from which life was made
spring forth from my broken heart.

Has not enough perseverance been produced?
And where is the hope, the spring, eternity?
Where have they taken my Lord?
I would fly with eagles

and not be weary of this world.
To sleep! To live in the arms of the angels
who come close to me in dreams…
I will rest and reconsider

whether perhaps I might hold fast
a little longer to the weeping, wandering
prophet's words and believe still
in this absent God who will not

let me go. Even as I release
stillborn dreams from this body
and resign from my position,
filled still with a starlight wonder

I walk on into the silent morning
and through this world's endless night,
caught up here in the Upside Down
only wishing to reside in something

that resembles the home within—
somewhere where all false stories
of who I am fall away, where there are
feathers and promises on the wind

and laughter in the light of love
that, in the dying dreams, overshadow
the long presence of pain and
set me free. At last,

in this home I have long envisioned,
this simple resting place, He comes
to meet me in the garden one day
and places his hand on my heart.

And then, after awhile, when I have
begun to see whatever it is I cannot see,
from his hand comes the Spirit dove
who leads us both to eternity.

Context

Where I come from,
and by that I mean originally,
one sees all; and thus, the need
for being rooted in singular perspective
is by nature irrelevant and inconsequential.
There is no such thing as irreparability.
And to think of context would simply
work against the infinitely expanding
meaning of a body of being
or bodies of gift ever in motion,
never parted from love.

In the moments
you perhaps remember judiciously
and think upon as misdeed
or rampant failure to be of fixed position
or find relevancy in casual causal consequence...
What you perceive as lack of contextuality
was evidence, bountifully, of true residence,
eternal belonging—the only
way of human being I knew
to heal, uplift or change false notion
of broken-hearted lone dove.

In my defense,
though I seemed to act precipitously
or fail to listen or heed
your presumed authority of my mission,

my soul did not inform my mind...
and my heart was with you; hence
I was lost in a system of partiality,
in seas of separation, drowning,
yet held to higher duty, being
suspended in rift with one devotion:

whole-hearted pure love
and loyalty.

In Egypt or in Greece

In Egypt or in Greece
and, if you dare to dream of
reversing shipwrecked dreams,
then off the coast of Sicily…

On Patmos and Peyrepreteuse
and by the Orb or somewhere
in the South of France where
we wish we may or might by chance

find some way to live and let live
and die to all the wars between us…
Or should it be in Avalon
where all things green and gone
shall spring to life again?

Ask me where or why or when.
I will come up with somewhere
there's a space and a place to be
all we were always meant to be,
which is just happy and free.

In the mountains or by a lake
in Italy—always back to Italy…
In Ireland by the sea or
in the Highlands or at the South Pole…

The Magda Poem Cycle

It matters not to me where
but that it happen on this
I will not relent. Whether still
existing here or heaven sent, I will
walk with you through time
and I will choose to live in love

and be on the way
with you.

The Magda Poem Cycle

Your Shame Is Not My Shame

How through the ages they placed upon her
all manner of restraints, dark devices diabolical,
failing nonetheless to strike silent the life
that lived through her and in time
seeing their own reflection in their practiced torture
and the tantamount truth of their own
tortured souls.

> *Your shame is not my shame.*
> I am not this monstrosity you made of me
> and she yet lives, free to return to the freedom
> that bore her through those ages.

How from one year to the next, undaunted, she rose
to do her best, to give her all, to find some rest,
to heed the call. And this it seemed
was something they deemed too much, their
misappropriation of her love blatant blasphemy
of all creation's light, a shattering
of peace-filled, day-born night.

> *Your shame is not my shame.*
> I will no more bend to all the barriers built,
> pyramids of projection that are mere inversion
> to save you from a cavernous ache of empty.

How this day there comes faint echo across these hills,
a whimpering turned to bloodthirsty howl

that would kill the owl and seize
and shake the very thing that might hold
the key to release them from their suffering.
She no longer shivers but walks in cool
clear rivers singing a freedom song.

Your shame is not my shame.

I choose to nurture the seed that yet grows
for the time of this life that remains and to be
who I am and have been and to begin again again.

Good Grief

Repeated there: patterned denial,
replicated reverberation of I alone,
naturally. In the reverence, a soliloquy—
song of solemnity, faintest remembrance.

I no longer recall first spring of sorrow;
the river only runs red in distant dreams.
And yet forever and the day bring me back
to knife's edge, my heart's open wound.

I carry on, for I am strong; this is how I have
always made it through, ever loyal to you,
which in a certain light seems mere folly,
a fine-tuned contrast to my exemplary fortitude.

And what do you see, sailor, great spirit,
survivor of the storm? Do you too view
yourself in a favorable light? Do you ever see
through the spyglass of time an image reversed?

It seems not. But who am I to say or even ask
this much of time and space, the illusionary light
of this dark age? Moored in a mirage, I am multiplication,
many-mirrored reflection of weakness to you.

And to myself I am a mere memory divided
into this indivisible truth: I am the river. I am
the dream, alive and flowing on the seas of time.
There is sweetness in the sorrow, a gift.

The Magda Poem Cycle

Oh, good grief, how you heal me.
You break me open, force me to be true
and in so doing lead me back to folly
and to fortitude, to we two who judge

so easily and fail to see what is written
in the ship's log, star date 2023: eloquent
and echoed invitation to light, to life, to love
in the blue beyond and infinity.

Evidences

> Evidence: (n) *"the available body of facts or information indicating whether a belief or proposition is true or valid"*

Trace now the contour of her shape.
Note its invisibility, but make no attempt to deny
its evidentiary effect on your experience or "reality".

Take note first of the way you obtained what you saw
as necessary to fulfill your duty, cover your tracks and provide—
and how you thought nothing of taking everything from her.

With that established and the knowing that she always knew
and still she gave only love to you, though hated all you chose
to do and the many ways it left so many lives in ruin...

Turn now to the hotel room: in the madness, some momentary
reconsideration, inexplicable intervention, a recognition—or
the night before last for that matter... perhaps that is easier?

Shall we return to the lakeshore of your youth? Or venture
further to you wading through dark waters in search of your sword
before you charmed the snake and so many others?

A million moments swirling in a multiplying mind, but then:
the butterfly and how she caught the coattails of your heart
and then all that opened up because and how you shut it down.

The Magda Poem Cycle

Or did you know how she, the advocate, argued on your behalf,
all while being halved by a pompous pauper set upon some
worldly throne and that she never wavered in all the years alone?

How she sent many gifts to the one you stated, irrefutably,
to be the owner of your lonely heart and turned aside
from all the arrows and never spoke a word against?

So as you sit there spinning, questioning the validity
and the viability of one who has offered only life or try to justify
the way you saw her through clouds of confusion you consumed
so willingly, like mashed potatoes served up scrumptiously,

would you check in again with your heart and how it fell apart?
But wait, do you not remember who sat with you in the dark
when your foot slipped upon the stair? Do you see where

she seemed to be in two places at once but never apart
from the truth and the life as she walked upon her way?
How many times had she been burned upon some stake

or left for dead or torn to pieces in one room or another
from which she had been excluded? So make your proposition
or do not, but surely you must abide by rubric of irrevocability.

Surely you see clearly your mind's infallibility in this case
and, if so, must erase nothing from the record and stand clean
before your God and all you say you stand for and see:

this body broken and also her spirit undeterred—and love: *alive!*
And life that cannot be extinguished and will not defy its right
to be in formation and ever in alignment with what remains.

Whatever is honorable, whatever is right, whatever is pure
and lovely and commendable, what is honest and just,
dwell now upon these things. **Remember** now what is true.

She Who Loves and Watches Over Me

Through time I trembled,
shrieking through flames,
remembering again how you left me:
you, who lived within my heart
raised whole armies to silence me,
turning them one by one
against me.

I lost full my mind,
but my heart she held,
reaching through time's fire to find me
and raise me up to new life.
I fly blind but she watches
through night into daybreak,
stands for me.

Back to Italy

Take me back to Italy
where you will make a different choice
and I will speak with my own voice
the words you could not receive,
did not believe, for I have
held them through these years
and let them live through all the tears.

Take me back to Italy.

I am back in Italy.
I write last letter from my cell,
so much still left to say, to tell.
You were and are man of your word—
no lines are blurred; yet,
you claimed my work as your own,
leaving to now no unturned stone,

left me there in Italy.

I can't go back to Italy,
though mem'ry fades as that last rose
you brought me, though not one soul knows
what happened but the morning birds
who have no words. Nor do I.

Yet still this story lives within,
and I wish to begin again
whether here or Italy.

There is no back to Italy
as it is here, not there, present,
tense, loving message we both sent
that life and light might be restored
love unleashed, poured
as healing rain replenishing.
I see now: we are finishing

what began in Italy.

Desert Moon

Ezekiel's wheel turns in June's deep sky and
so much time has passed now between us.

We approach the midpoint of another turning year,
well into the journey of our great return.
A summer sun shines, resplendent from within,
and I wonder at the revelation, long to see.

I remember still where we came from.
I remember still where we have been.

There are so many stories that cannot be contained
I release them now and surrender to night,
share this little light, feel full this ocean love,
and rest in knowing there is no more to do, just be.

I remember what we came here for.
I remember where we have yet to go.

Still, without you, I fly blind but now at last see
the stillness in the storm I am has remained.
So tonight I light a candle, blow it out;
in the flame, in the breath, in this day, am free.

This tired heart, an open book unread,
glows bright for you beneath a desert moon.

The Wreckage Lies Behind

The wreckage lies behind
and still there is sacred work to be done.
There are greater seas for us to sail. *Can you see?*

Lay down your sword and all these things
you think to be so urgent and important.
Drink now from this sacred cup and rest.
Reclaim clarity. Release ambiguity.

All these battles you have fought for all you believe.
Make way now for all your heart would conceive
this time with faith and without compromise.
Reclaim humility. Release all incivility.

There are greater seas for us to sail. *Can you see?*
While still there is sacred work to be done,
the wreckage lies behind.

Where We Meet Again

Reflected by the water's edge the brittle branch
is alive and echoes the story of how far we have come,
the one below, reflected and pushing upward, using all
the strength she never knew she had, and the one above,
swooping gracefully and touching grace, finding gentleness
he never knew to be his own.

Our lilac love alive after all these years—
and so much that seemed dead to the both of us.
We are deep water and mystical earth, meeting
at the surface, not knowing what might yet be born
within this new song rising up to life as we create
heaven's home within our mirrored hearts.

Like lightning that does no harm but merely
illuminates, expands and lightens all, releasing
all that would corrupt the purity of our shared light
made manifest, we are lit with truth and have come
so close and heard the night's thunderous applause
reverberating in twin hearts made whole.

All turns to magic, multiplied and blossoming
into something we never even thought to imagine:
a silvery possibility so beautiful and wrapped in mystery
that we are elevated in a three-stranded spiral and
transcend all that seemed in the breath before
impossible. The world once closed off opens up.

Here where we meet again, we let it be and welcome
the preservation of all that remains: Love set free
because we found faith. We rise up and merge our shared truth
into new wineskins, pouring out hope upon the nations. For this
is why I have plumbed the depths, why you have come back to life,
why we have found our way back to beginning again.

If I Have to Move Mountains

If I have to move mountains then so be it.
Let the mountains move and the red seas part
because I intend to walk at least half way.

Faith to faith, across oceans of forgiveness
I will meet you if you dare to make this journey.
There is so much we do not know.

We must honor the other's grief,
the shared suffering of separate lives
and hold a space beneath the shaded tree.

I've been planting mustard seeds for years
and all the birds upon my branches
are ready now to fly.

You, beautiful dreamer, still as bold as ever,
have moved mountains more than I,
were blind as I. But now we see.

This much I believe.

Shall I Go to India

Shall I go to India,
to the valley where they say
I was meant to be born
and find the cave, which is,
perhaps, the only place I
would not remember you?

Or would I only think of you
and every choice you made
that denied what was meant to be
for me then? Would I be
chased there, too, by
grave ghosts of your past

And take yet another
high road that leads to yet
another year gone in the blink
of an eye? Might I lose myself
in the swirl of confusion but
see your smile everywhere,

and remember standing here
ten thousand years, alone
in one place or another?
Would I follow the sound
of his remembered laugh
only to have it lead me back

to the picture of the Romani man
and the cascade of my ancient tears?
Shall I live in the ashram or
dance to the freedom flute?
Wherever I go, there I am—
and you… you are everywhere.

I Will Shoot No Arrows

About last night
and your impulse to incite,
the compulsion to flee or fight,
and at all costs to be right,

I will shoot no arrows.
I have no messages of love
or angry missives to condemn.
I will stand and will not fall

for such self-compromise and denial
of the one soul from which we come,
now washed clean of dirty deed,
Spirit reclaiming wasted seed

and restoring again and again
what either one of us seeks to eradicate.
This morning the sun rose beautiful
across the glassy lake,

where all I see is the love beneath,
life's true reflection of purity.
So here I stand in silent reverie,
untouched, untainted, unmovable

as Spirit has fixed me
to the one star we are.

Stacks of Books

When you came to Rome the first time
and found me writing by candlelight,
you and I talked forever about
my stack of books and all the stories
I would try to write.

But time swept away the stories
and you were swept up in a story, too,
and we lost everything before
I had the chance to give you true story
of our great love.

On the desk in your room here: your stack
of books, all of them familiar to me,
like you, a man larger than life, the one
I knew I came to find again,
lost already.

Foreshadowed grief saw me standing
months later in the hall, where you balanced
stack of books on one hand, staring
through me again when I said I did not
see or understand.

The Magda Poem Cycle

For many years I sat alone
sans speech or emotion, burying myself
in a stack of books, seeking to
remember, remember what you forgot
but I could not.

Then, another decade gone,
I rose from yet another shipwreck night, spent,
began to write and paint and try
to go on. So here I sit surrounded
by more stacks of books.

It means so little without you.
All I can think is what I cannot do
alone and how time is slipping and
all the stacks of books we've yet to write
with our great love.

There Is More

You always prized yourself
on being fair and how many times
I said you were because in your heart you are.

But in review it isn't true. You played people
like chess pieces—you up there in your chair
pretending to be the Great Mover, seeing the rest of us
through eyes ever fixed on imaginary prize, some reward
bestowed for grand achievement, generous magnanimity
that was mere distraction from deep bereavement
and all the lost things hemorrhaging
from one heart and mind.

Maybe you never even knew
what it was you would do, dismantling
the psyches of those who fell in line for you,
not to mention all the players who showed up in your life
as friend or foe, lover or wife, parent, child, free and wild
or meek and mild, and I—the one you cast as deviant defiant.

Our lessons each identical: to rise above being compliant.
You so close to God yet led astray, forgetting now
what it meant to walk in the Way.
Or worse—remembering it by heart
and severing it nevertheless at the start,

Sacrificing Truth for your little lie
that opened the door to so much more.

The Magda Poem Cycle

I know you see it still as some race well run
and it is true so much good has been done.
But at what cost? And what was lost
in your insistence on authority (not to mention
authorship for you or whomever you chose to give it to).

Do you not hear the drip, drip, drip coming from
your well-traveled but ever sinking ship?
You, great conquerer through time, supposed
discoverer of this, freedom's fine land,
and in another time arbiter of its truth.

Do what once you did and leave that boat.
Tear down that iron wall, ancient moat
you built sturdy around your heart,
cementing yourself in until
death do us part again and again,
all in pretended dedication
to a calling, to a cause
and separation of that from Love.

But he is not a cause,
and least of all the cause for such a choice
for suffering. He is the life, the way, the truth,
and it is truth that sets you free.

For freedom we were set free.
This you whispered there and then.
This I believed in Italy.... believe it still.

So today as you are climbing up that hill,
stop to rest and listen, listen, listen in
for the heartbeat of remembrance.

Eat your bread. Drink your wine.
Recall a fairer time when I was by your side,
friend or foe, lover, bride. See me now as
something more than some feather
in your cap, a means to an end,
the rotten apple discarded,
forgotten friend.

Find me in your very core.
Hear me whispering,
"There is more."

After the Storm

There will be a shipwreck
and you will face the stormy sea
and think it may swallow you whole
and the storm take all those
you have so loved.

But take heart, my love.
Try to see, to remember
only the best moments,
even if you have wholly
forgotten me.

You will yet live.

I remember it as if it were
yesterday—never mind the seas of time.
Your ship had sailed by then and when
it happened I did not know as I
fled to the forest, alone. Yet,
through the wind's howl
I prevailed and ever,
for whatever reason,
believed in you,
wanted you
to live

In spite of all the death
and even in moments
that became years
when I could not
catch my breath.

I would yet live.

Though you had taken everything from me
before you sailed back home, then again
loaded the ship so methodically
and like a captain called his crew,
inspiring them in the way you do...

Still I held you in my heart
and, when I saw the storm
that came for you, somehow
found the strength to stand
and beg for mercy, admittedly
as much for me as for you.

It was the only hope to keep
any hope alive in me:
to honor what was also true
which was my love for you.

You will yet speak to Caesar.
You will make it back to Italy
though I may not.

The Magda Poem Cycle

And what of freedom?
What of love?

This I whispered as I drowned
in my own sea of sorrow, lost
to myself. My spirit gave out and birds
flew fast to me and sang me to sleep.

Three days passed and I wailed,
caught up in a nightmare
that was all too real:
the Teacher, gone,
the Child, gone.
You, gone.

I did not want to live
but God did exactly
what he said he would
and kept me alive too.

I saw your ship sink
and with this my heart sank too
and I retreated to the cave. I did not
know for years whether not only I
but the world had lost you.

All was darkness.
All was night.

Though I would not see you, I heard the stories
and my heart found a sliver of something good
in the way you cut loose the precious cargo
and without the light of sun or stars
knowing the ship would be cast
upon some rocky shore, remembered
the light of God in you.

And I rejoiced in the Lord—
always holding on somehow
to this one thing at least
we still shared.

Look, love, what happened then:
Spain! And all the rains across the plains
mainly were mild. All the rivers ran wild.
You had your moment of triumph
before the bitter end five years
after the storm spit you out
on the distant shore.

The news came to me too late
in that day, in that age, and
the world did lose you as I had.

And what now of freedom?
What of love?

The Magda Poem Cycle

Here and now we have our Neros
and those who practice treachery,
anarchy, and debauchery, who inflict
acrimony and agony. And there you are,
having survived a storm. I see you
building a proverbial fire, just trying
to rekindle the flame of faith.
No viper that emerges
may harm you.

Rest now, if you must.
Make whatever house you're in
your home and keep the faith, my love.
Your story does not end in this storm.

Unhindered by fury or fire
I have no doubt you will rise up
like a lion in my heart.
And whether you sail again
or take up the pen in this new day,
the dawn of this new era,

There is but one thing
I wish to know:

What now of freedom?
What of love?

News of Your Release

That summer I had waited for news of your release.
I was so certain you would make your way
back to the valley and home to me.

Shipwrecks and entanglements notwithstanding,
nor the Greek nor the one who held your pursestrings—
least of all the Holy Roman Empire

would stand in your way. This is what I would say
when they begged me not to believe in second chances
or made me think choosing you meant

breaking my vow to him. But that we always shared,
you and I, and there was nothing left to lose except to choose
a love that was larger than my life or yours.

Did you know, before you died, that I already had
chosen you. That my dream never died. And so when I
stood outside the walls in the place you stood

and wished I could go back in time or make some sense
of a life so full of losses, I saw it all—the story as I would
have written it, the life we might have lived.

And it was beautiful. It was good. And then I blinked
and I was a girl whose knees gave way and stumbled
walking on those same stones

The Magda Poem Cycle

Two thousand years in the future, my father's face
before me speaking of our distant story—
yours with his words, mine with his heart—
and I was overcome.

With madness, some would later say. Or fantasy.
It is all the same to me and means nothing in the light
of a love that cannot be contained by time.

Riveted back to the memory of she who lived in me
and her love for you, one nobody knew or would believe,
I saw her journey on from this cold place that summer.

She (is it I?) would leave soon after to climb another mountain,
far away on an isle called Patmos to write of how it was
in the beginning for him and in the end for every one of us,

to bid him come quickly and do not tarry. But I left
one part out of the vision and the story, which is
both fact and allegory. I did not say

that I saw you, too, far in the distance but walking toward me
with the boy, a river of sparkling forgiveness that ran both ways
and became a fleur-de-lis fountain where we met

in the middle of time and with no need for words.
The thought of it now makes me break out in laughter—
that you and I, both who always wanted the last word,

could have no need for them at all. Twelve again
in this lifetime, I got up with clear direction
from he who had come as he said he would.

He told me it was time to remember and to hold
these treasures in my heart. Had I known
all the ways that would tear me apart

I would have laughed at him. But his laughter and yours…
they always come back to me and they say one thing
and the same: *There is a way….*

There is a way, and the gate is narrow.
It is said that so few find it. I wonder if we missed it.
What can I do but wait for news of your release

and pray you remember me and take us back
to Italy or maybe far away and into a better day,
here and now, set free to love again.

All Ships Have Sailed

Soon I will sail into the West
again on clean-up duty
for the mess I had no part in making
and all you left in shambles
while you pretended to take notes
on the matter you created
and all that was ended.

If I do not sound elated, well,
such astute assessment is correct.
Truth will not be negated,
notwithstanding ways you dissect
it as experimental and play
the dancing juggler so focused
on life's messages rescinded.

All ships have sailed.
What love had prevailed
despite all the heinous acts
has now been swept away to sea
and all that leaves is me
awash in seas full of plastic,
life polluted by your pretense.

Hence, this poem and my focus
while you practice hocus-pocus
and praise the false feminine
granting nine lives while

secretly throwing knives
and going round and round,
killing time and putting off

seeing yourself stranded there
sinking slowly into the dawning awareness
that all ships have sailed.
No man is an island,
and you've no foundation for
the falsity bought out and built up
brick by lifeless brick.

But this hard truth in this
just-the-facts poetic justice does not
erase the love with which he loves
and all the rivers running to you
that will fill this earth with a shaking joy
when at last we bring you home,
back to where you belong.

The light of day comes quickly
and the advent of awakening approaches
from the East and new beginnings
even where you thought all things were dead
and gone, long buried or erased from the record.
I know I sound like a broken one, but again I say,
all ships have sailed. Make your way home

into the light of a thousand stars,
shining in the one true light not only in name
but as one with it, allowing the waters to rise
and fall down to cleanse you, to part you
from all the stories you created once upon
a time before this terrible, truth-filled time.

In the end, we begin.
Are you ready?

The Magda Poem Cycle

In the Shadow of My Mountains

When you stood there,
in the shadow of my mountains,
in all likelihood at the very point that is my center point
did you know I was meant to be there
by the lake on that very day?

Did you hear the mighty roar
of my Anabaptist ancestors splashing in the waters
just beneath the bridge you crossed? Did you get
disoriented and turned around in the place
where I once got lost?

And did you know where God led me to
on this the day of your beginning, the longest
day I used to hate because I would fall apart
and turn myself inside out just to try
to figure out why you cut me out

and off from everything,
banished me and then my little boy, too.
"For no reason at all" he used to repeat endlessly
in the years I had no words or food to feed him
and my mind had gone blank. I was

somewhere lost in time. But now
I am found and grateful to have been
resuscitated, raised up from the icy waters
to face the astonishing truth
of how long I have loved you.

The Magda Poem Cycle

I have faced it and faced it
and I will face it again I am sure.
Face down in my pillow, there are no tears, only
a half-smile that for at least a little while
you have been happy again.
I am grateful for all that has been
and for the castle on the hill. I can hear

Ed Sheeran singing the song. There you are.
On the boat. And again in the restaurant.
Did you go there again this time?

It's real, you know. I know you
will know what you know in time even
if I've given up on time and set my life on fire
or retreated once more into silence.
Still, I will love you.

I will speak truth. And I will
believe, because once upon a time
you made me believe when you said I had a future and,
despite your precise provision of
every evidence to the contrary,

this much I know is true.
And so all is well. Love is patient,
love is kind. Love withstands all wrongs. I will lay down
my head to rest now, this candle burning
in my heart as I sing a lullaby,

Beatles style, of course...
and dream of my dream come true,
served up by the maker of the stars in every detail
save one and I will fall to sleep tonight
and wonder who will meet me

by the sea, on the mountain,
in the valley where we tumbled like little children
laughing and then fell asleep together
after I sang you a birthday song
long ago. So long.

All That Shall Not Be Taken

And what of choosing the better part?
Here it means nothing. This has been
my life's persistent scream,
demand for one thing.

I plead my case...

People chasing after you…
They slow down for the drive-by,
arm themselves with evidence,
then draw their unwieldy swords,
reckless with their newfound truth
and hammer, hammer away
with all their trite reasons why
one must get up, *try, try, try*.

And more insistent:

When you sent them two by two
and taught us the Law of Love
did you know one thing only:
that I would be so lonely?
When you broke the bread in two,
dipped it in the blood-red wine,
did you see what was to come—
tit for tat, their zero-sum?

He answers now.

And what of choosing the better part?
This is everything. This has been
my life's persistent dream,
release of one thing.

Touching my face...

Begin at the end again:
He greeted me with a kiss,
Judas in the olive grove...
and Peter's sword—he so quick
to defend and to pretend.
Taste of vinegar sour,
your wide eyes piercing my soul,
all that was broken, made whole.

I no more resistant...

Is this beginning an end?
For I have known traitor-friend
who by cover of night came
and here Peter multiplied,
ever appearing beside,
still unwieldy with his sword.
Here they call you Savior, Lord;
Love's one truth tattered, ignored.

I ask him now:

What remains? To choose again?
To live, to breathe, to dance and sing?
What is not taken? Love's lighted gleam?
The two as one thing?

He smiles and speaks.

All that remains is to begin again—
your heart's offering,
what's freely given: radiant beam,
three in one, life's ring.

One Last Ship

Was it your goodbye
to the life you had once thought
to be your ticket to freedom—
on one last ship
before the wreck
before Rome
before I
was forced to say
my last goodbye
alone
at the stone
where they placed
your severed head?

Or was that trip some
celebration instead,
a reaffirmation of the perfect ending
that had no place for me—
even after all the years
apart, you cutting off my love
to spite your heart,
play the valiant part
after all
the believing your mind's story
of what was meant to be
and what was not.

The Magda Poem Cycle

Did you ever stop to consider
that one man's Camelot
is another woman's Hell?

In the end—what did you
tell the writer then?
Do not worry that your scribe
in such a hurry never
delivered last letter you wrote.
I know it by heart
and have carried it through time.
It is mine.

I hold no grudge against you.
Still I wonder,

Is it your last goodbye
to the life you had once thought
to be your ticket to freedom—
on one last ride
before what's next?
I pray for
some different end
before I
am forced to say again
my last goodbye
alone
at the stone that
only God can roll away.

Or is your trip some celebration instead,
a reaffirmation of the perfect ending
that has no place for me—
even after all the years
apart, you cutting off my love
to spite your heart,
play the valiant part
after all
the believing your mind's story
of what was meant to be
and what was not.

Did you ever stop to consider
that one woman's heartbreak life
is another man's slice of heaven?

These Three Remain

Great Gothic Spire, consumed by fire, what stories have you
yet to tell? For whom the bell tolls
ask not and neither cry.

Five thousand miles away, Three Churches fell to flames as you,
their steeples reach no more to sky.
Their people sing outside.

Souls of all We Who Mourn so great a loss and count the cost
stand witness to the rage and ruin
and all that is unknown.

Did the Blessed Mother throw open compassionate arms,
gathering up citizens of
City of Lights and Love?

Did the Maid of Orléans turn again to face the fire,
repeating for a second time,
Jesus Jesus Jesus!

Did Magda, forgotten there, become the burning tower,
rise from ash and fight fire to fire,
a phoenix, Holy Flame?

The Magda Poem Cycle

When the Rose Windows nearly shattered, did heaven shudder
and scatter a thousand pale petals
to heal and remind us:

Three good graces yet remain: Wonder, Mystery, Beauty.
These form a Threefold Trinity.
Faith, Hope, and Love below

Rise to join three in one Father, Son, and Holy Spirit
in Sacred Union with Mother, Daughter, and Shekinah—
at last one star complete.

Sing out, you who have no home and feel the heart's burning pain!
Raise your voice to find Love's lost song.
Know now: Our Lady reigns.

Come quickly now, you Mighty Lion, Son of truth divine.
Your bride awaits, adorned, prepared
to meet you on your way.

Take flight, You Freedom Warriors!
Rest your wings upon the wind.
Rise now to be the Light set free
in love! Come back to life...

> *Back to life*
> *Back to life*
> *Back to life*

Laid Bare

Blindfolded and bound beneath
their pointed swords
she saw no better choice
than to have no part
of their wretched game,
the bloody knives
and tainted coins
all their clanging,
clashing, banging,
bashing—all while
the red river ran
through time, taking
with it the father's own child
clothed by the sun and innocent.

The dragon, red, relentless
in his pursuit
of her pure character
loosed upon the land
cutting off the hand
reaching for food
hungry for love.
As skies turn green,
no hope is seen.
On the red field
the left and the right
keep up their fight
and nobody sees her there,
her heart battered, broken, laid bare.

On the Way

All those years ago
when I gave up playing the role
in which you and others so willingly cast me
and threw off all the clothes I never wanted to wear
in this life that only served to cloak me in some hope
of protection, after I had cried the torrential river for two years
and then succumbed to being struck mute
and forced to hear, receive the Word of God
that is my sustenance, the bread of life
and living water that sustains me,
there came a moment of clarity when I
laid down my silver sword of light
and asked only to be healed.

Surrendering everything,
I asked God to gather up whatever whirlwind
it might take to remove all that was in the way.
I prayed that all my idols might fall or be seized
complete. I stopped trying to put myself in
what seemed to me to be "the right place" or "the right time"
which usually meant to my heart anywhere in the vicinity
of yours in whatever dimension I traversed.
I got down on my knees, for hours or days,
even months at a time. I waited,
sitting Job-like in the ruin and shambles
of all the towers crashing and the life that
seemingly never came to be.

The Magda Poem Cycle

And when the debris
was finally swept away by the deluge
and there were the wasteland years,
when all day every day all I could hear
was the echo of my heart's cry for some friend,
some safe place to lay my head, I returned to all the only
true things—to the One as reflected in Spirit when I walked
again in the garden with him
or knelt before the throne,
as reflected in Truth and
my abiding love for you.

I took communion in nature
and learned to trust life in every moment,
letting go of the things of this world
that had never been my home anyway
and finding solace with the birds of the air,
the lilies of the field. And one day I was happy.
Heaven came down as it rose from my heart
with the dawning realization that all things
are possible and true things rise up in the time
ordained long before our presence here.

Before me now, from within my green-field heart,
rainbow roads spiral out in every direction,
and I see that all roads will lead me home.
When I meet with obstacles or lay down in the rain,
still saddened by the loss of the one I treasure
most of all as true friend, it is only to rest and regain
my strength, for I know God will lift me up

and I will walk on, for this is the journey
my soul came here to make. When I think
you or any other cares not, simply because
you are missing in action in my life, I pause
and remember that you and they are ever-present
in the infinite field of expanding love and grace
and I am held there eternally,

Seen for who I am there, if not here,
I am preparing the way for my heart to see
with new eyes here and lead my life with love.
I no longer know where I am going but still
I follow, traversing the territory of the soul
and the unpredictability of this life on Earth.
Some days I have no strength. Wandering
in circles or simply sitting in silence by the lake alone,
my heart retraces all the steps I have taken here.
But, like this poem, it flows on like water,
slipping from my grasp as do all those
I have most loved and longed for,
knowing and trusting all the same
that you are with me,
have been always,
on the way.

All the Things I Know Nothing Of

For so long I observed the world
and tried to adapt to its customs, looking for meaning
and seeming to find none by its standards,
casting myself off like a forgotten thing,
my trust in what I knew by heart waning
in the bright lights and shiny seasons
that seemed to pass me by.

I made notes about the little things,
how one should know what one does in the world
and not only who one is beneath the suit, how
you ask about another's day, how happy
birthday wishes and Christmas cards
arriving in the mail meant I
had not been forgotten.

I will never forget how I held your card
and imagined you remembered more than I had
thought you did and how that sparked
me again, like the words you spoke,
like the way you looked out on the water
from the boat, like the way you float
and fly through dreams with me.

I dreamed the dream I dreamed was true
for you, and I suppose I came to believe in time
you would find the words or let it be
as it has always been and not pretend.

But I was most true in the beginning
of this life, untainted by all the
little expectations, all the incantations
and proclamations that rang hollow
in my heart.

I chose the dream, the dance, the dare
to be free of all such things. Sometimes,
as I await the advent and second birth,
singing to myself in a language
only I know, I am like a little child,
not knowing anything, scooping up
all the things I know nothing of, holding
them in love.

I set free all I thought I knew. They died
and lived again the day I sat across from you
after signing your petition for my absence,
betraying everything for nothing, thinking
this demand would be your last, never
dreaming of all the wintry blasts
yet to come or of all the silent nights—
but also never imagining that so many
miracles would come to pass.

Who can say when our hearts and souls
are reborn on earth where the road will lead,
whether we will fail or succeed in some
attempt to remember or forget, to soar
or as before to fly below some imagined radar?
Who can say when we choose to walk in the way
of love what will be?

Who can say what star might rise in the East
on the bleakest midwinter night or who might
appear, bearing the unexpected gift, breaking forth
like a Son who enters in to the heart's chamber
and holds you like a little child, smiles
and says, "Well done"? No one knows
the hour and so we await again
the revelation of a mystery.

Michael, Mary, and Me

Michael, the Archangel
and Mary, Mary my mother,
his mother, your mother,
our mother—

Both have been holding me
so close, guarding me
and guiding me,
carrying me,

Telling me they will take me
to where I'm meant to be
even if I've collapsed
here so close

To the place where we
meet again, begin again
here at the end.
I have been crying

Because for so many years
I have stood strong,
knowing in the longing for
even I belong,

No matter all the cutting off
from everyone and every
place that mattered to me.
Now I am a babe

Born again into this love
and still alone while you roam.
And still unable to bring forth
all the love that rushes through,

Asking the angels where are you
who promised me so very long ago
that if I held strong and kept my pledge
they would bring support I need.

Now all has fallen in.
All has fallen through.
I have fallen down, down
and out and back into

the arms of grace,
eternal waiting place.

The Coming Age Now Here
The Magda Poem Cycle
Fall and the Color of Change

A Tick Tock Truth

She swings in the balance
of a tick tock truth
counting down the swings
back and forth, back and forth
until the lid's blown off.

It's game on because time's up
and there's no rewind
down on planet earth
where it's fast forward, fall
fast toward Elysian.

First the underbelly—
good society's
dirty money scam
brought forth, sickness spit out:
wretched rank remorse.

See! Life hath no fury
on these storm-tossed seas.
He will calm the storm
when we have eyes to see
him standing on the shore.

What more? How much lower
do we wish to go?
Bobbling to and fro
not wanting to believe
in heaven or in hell.

Who can tell the story's
depth, depravity
disguised as glory?
Divided increments
of time buried beneath.

Rising up from the grave
where they buried her
she calls forth angels
of innocence restored,
heaven's sacred rest.

Shot in the Heart, He Returns the Arrow of Love

The age of normalcy
and all such fickle fallacy
has passed.

The Great Return is not
to normal, new or not; there's not
a standard average doled out—
that is not what Love's about.

Your bribery may fill
the coffers of deceivers, still
there will come a reckoning,
requisite reordering.

The Age of Mystery
and miracles is coming soon,
not just a shot of "reality"
and far more than practicality.

Place now your hand on heart,
no pledge of allegiance required,
present and accounted for,
loved no matter choice you make.

The age of clemency
is a mercy, a healing
grace for all.

Walls Come Tumbling Down: After Revolution

The world is filled with the clucking
of people who copy what they see
and proclaim it perfectly pure.

But the revolution will be a reckoning
and the fulfillment of the prophecy
they preach. Love will win the day.

And, make no mistake: the truth will stand.
Still, all will see author's hand of originality,
startled by resonant ring of authenticity.

Echoes of effability, eloquent explanation,
matter not in the light of Love's insistent illumination.
Politics of the polite and performance aside,

All manner of falsehood will be made known,
the scroll opened to the trumpet's clarion call,
and the walls come tumbling down.

What Must Be Faced

The time of
plausible deniability
has come to a close.
The chain of command

is broken and the straw man
will be sacrificed in their scurry
to cover their tracks as they
tuck their tails and run.

But there is no place to hide
from the truth made plain
no matter the pain
that now must be faced

by every one of us once immersed
in the lives we loved and the convenience
we accepted in exchange
for believing a lie.

May the anger be acknowledged
and released without endless bargaining.

May we hold our sadness softly without lapsing
into the chasm of depression or the long dark night.

May we move in due time to accept what has
happened here and know again what it means
to live free.

www.ingramcontent.com/pod-product-compliance
Lightning Source LLC
Chambersburg PA
CBHW060532080526
44586CB00012B/707